Conrad K. Butler

ANIMALS ALL AROUND:

Incredible and funny facts

Koala leads a rather slow lifestyle, not making much effort with its activity (despite everything, in case of danger, it can run away quickly). It is worth noting, however, that this animal spends almost the entire day (from 19 to 22 hours) simply ... sleeping. Nay. The koala actually doesn't even mind where and in what position it sleeps, so it fully deserves to be called the biggest lazy animal.

Penguins propose to their mate just like humans. The difference is that we give our chosen one an engagement ring, which is a symbol of our love, while penguins give their beloved ... a pebble. The selected specimen must be nice, smooth, large and shiny, so that it seems the most attractive to the one who will accept it. Because a female penguin, just like a woman, can also reject the proposal if the candidate does not make an effort. If, on the other hand, she likes the gift, she will express her "yes" by putting it in the nest.

We often don't realize how surprising some animals can be. Curiosities from their world can surprise us, such as the extraordinary regenerative abilities of snails. These inconspicuous creatures do not have to worry when they accidentally lose an eye. Although it sounds completely unbelievable, it will simply grow back after some time and will function in the same way as the previous ones. This is certainly a practical solution that many people may not have realized.

I don't think any of us like being sick. Sometimes we get tired then for a long time, fighting with nausea and abdominal pain. However, the frog copes with it much better than the human. How? When it swallows something that can irritate its digestive tract, an insect such as an ant or a wasp, it immediately regurgitates its stomach. It then cleans it out of the body and swallows it back. It must be admitted that this is an excellent method in the fight against indigestion.

It's worth taking a closer look at the crocodile. We usually associate it with a huge appetite and an equally huge threat. Meanwhile, this animal can do very well without food. It is certainly astonishing, however, an adult crocodile may not eat quietly for about a year, waiting for a favorable opportunity. Why? Well, these animals have a much slower metabolism than, for example, humans and, at the same time, low energy requirements. This is certainly one of the features that allow this species to survive, even in very unfavorable conditions.

Although the cow is one of the most popular farm animals, it holds some secrets that most of us have no idea about. Bearing in mind curiosities from the animal world, it is worth paying attention to how strong bonds cows can create between themselves. In their communities, they find, like us, best friends with whom they stick all the time. However, when two friendly individuals are separated, it can result in their worse well-being and even depression. This proves how sociable and sensitive they are.

Every cat lover who eagerly discovers interesting facts about pets may be surprised to know that beautiful, tortoiseshell fur is almost exclusively reserved for females. Tortoiseshell fur is a combination of two colors - most often red and black (although black can also be replaced by another color, for example blue or chocolate). If you meet a cat with a beautiful, spotted tortoiseshell coloration (although there are also point and tabby coats), you can be almost 100% sure that you are dealing with a female cat, as tortoiseshell males are a real rarity.

Horned Phrynoma is an inconspicuous lizard from the Phrynosomatidae family. A small, and at the same time not very pretty creature, it resembles a horned toad with a short tail. What natural curiosities about animals are associated with this strange reptile? A surprising fact about his life is a unique protective system. When threatened, the lizard puffs ominously to increase its volume and make a more menacing appearance. However, if this method proves to be unreliable, the reptile gushes blood from the pores located in the corners of the eyes.

The Brookesia micra chameleon is a charming and at the same time microscopic creature, because its length, including the tail, is only 30 mm! The animal, originally from Madagascar, was discovered between 2003 and 2007, and formally described in 2012. Apart from its surprising size, this lizard is not much different from other chameleons - the reptile can move its eyes independently of each other, thanks to which it does not have to turn its head to see everything that is happening around it perfectly. The pet also picks up ultraviolet light.

Among the birds, an unusual specimen is the Common Swift (Apus Apus). It's hard to believe, but it can stay in the air continuously for over 2 years. Are you wondering how this is possible? Jerzyk Zwyczajny developed such a tactic that when he feels tired, he ascends to an altitude of over 3,000 meters (3,280 yards) and glides freely, taking short naps.

The biggest killer of people among animals is ... a mosquito. It is estimated that more than 2 million people die from them every year. However, you must realize that the mosquito itself is not a killer - it alone will not kill us. So what is the reason? They are carriers of many dangerous diseases. The tiger mosquito from Asia has a particularly bad reputation.

Killer whales (Orcinus orca) are the most successful hunters in the animal kingdom. In their natural environment, they have no enemies, and thanks to their great strength and incredible intelligence, they can hunt down any victim. They prey not only on penguins, walruses, sea turtles and sharks, but also on whales. How is it possible that orcs are able to kill such a large animal? This is due to a clever strategy - when they track down the victim, they bite off its tongue and wait for it to bleed out.

"Rock, Paper, Scissors" is one of the simplest games. There is no doubt, however, that the concept of its principles requires the use of logical and abstract thinking. A human can handle it easily, but an animal? Well, yes. Chimpanzees are able to master this game at the level of a 4-year-old child.

Observing a giraffe during a meal, it is easy to see that these huge animals do not feed for very long next to one tree. Trees do not want to be eaten at all, so they have developed a number of mechanisms to protect them from herbivores. One of them is the secretion of bitter tannin, the smell of which reaches the next trees like an alarm signal. That's why giraffes feed against the wind and move on to the next tree before the warning signal reaches it.

It's no secret that cats have good eyesight. They only need 1/6 of the light that the human eye needs to see. They can see in a much wider field and can even see UV rays. It turns out, however, that cats are unable to see what is below the line... of their noses.

Sea otters are small animals that spend most of their time in the water. It is well known that it is in it that they relax or eat. What is interesting, however, is that they also sleep in the water! For people, this may seem unusual - after all, water is a place where it is easy to drown while sleeping. Well, for sea otters this is not a problem - they have a way to keep them from getting lost. It is holding hands while sleeping. This keeps them from separating and they are never alone when they wake up. The behavior of marine animals of this kind is extremely touching!

Did you know that whales are the largest mammals in the world? And this is how feeding one of their species - humpback whale - takes place. He can drink about 72 liters of milk a day. On the other hand, humpback whale milk is pink in color and contains as much as 50% fat.

The existence of bees on our planet is essential. These small insects pollinate plants while collecting nectar and pollen. Thanks to their work, e.g. vegetables and fruits not only produce more crops, but also the fruits produced by the plant are larger and prettier. Bees provide food not only for us, but thanks to them, animals also have food. Diadasia diminuta bees sleep in spheromalva flowers. They spend about 5-8 hours a day on rest. This is very important as it has been proven that tired bees have difficulty getting into their hive.

Moles are nearly blind: their tiny eyes are almost completely insensitive to light. However, they have extremely sensitive hearing, which allows them to find insects, larvae and earthworms underground. This is facilitated by the fact that they are creatures that move extremely fast underground. In just one day, it can dig up to 15 meters of corridors.

We all think that the laziest creature is the sloth.
However, it is far from the salamander living in
the caves of the Dinaric Mountains in the Balkans.
This salamander moves on average ... once every
7 years. In 2010, 19 specimens were captured, marked
and released back. Most of them moved less than
10 m (393 in) and one of them was in exactly the
same place.

The gorilla is so strong that it can lift 10 times its body weight. The ant... is stronger than him. It can lift 50 times its own body weight. However, the real record holder in this field is the dung beetle (the one that rolls balls). It has been calculated to move a weight that is more than 1,100 times its weight - if a human were that strong, I could lift about 85 tons.

It has been known for a long time that ravens, one of the smartest animals on our planet, can plan their breakfast for the next day and know how to get to hidden treats. Complicated social relationships are possible because these birds communicate in a very advanced way. For example, they can repeat the gesture meaning "look at it" until they get the attention of a companion. This proves that ravens are at least on the same level of intellectual development as chimpanzees.

A dog's nose print is unique and just as unique as a human fingerprint. Furrows and wrinkles in combination with the drawing of dog nostrils create an individual and individual imprint. This is a unique feature of each dog. For this reason, fingerprints are used to establish a person's identity. The same methods can be applied to a canine friend, identifying him by the imprint of his nose mirror.

Oysters are a species of molluscs that is characterized by high variability. These species are widely distributed in all shallow salt seas of the warm and temperate zones. During life, it changes sex, a male individual after a few weeks becomes female, and then returns to male sex – depending on current needs.

Dolphins, like no other animal, have mastered the art of staying alert and keeping their surroundings safe. Their vigilance and highly developed survival instinct show animal behavior. First of all, dolphins sleep with only one eye closed. Thanks to this, with the help of the other, they can control what is happening in their environment. In addition, one hemisphere of their brain remains active, which means that they do not lose control of their breathing.

Pigs are very sociable animals. Few people know about it, but they can communicate sympathy or hunger. They can express different emotions and states through 20 grunts and squeals. In addition, pigs respond to the names people give them. They are able to learn various tricks. They can, among others: herd sheep, jump over objects, roll carpets, fetch, bow.

Squirrels may be small, but they play a vital role in our environment, and one so important you may find it hard to comprehend. These little furry friends plant thousands of trees around the world every year, simply by forgetting where they hid their acorns.

A study was conducted at the University of Berlin to investigate what happens in the human brain when we are tickled. Tests on rats have shown that they actually enjoy being tickled as well, especially their backs. When tickled, rats make an extremely high-pitched sound similar to laughter. They even seek the experimenter's hand when they stop and ask for more!

The giant Pacific octopus is an extraordinary creature. With three hearts, nine brains and blue blood, these eight-armed creatures are nothing but aliens. One brain controls their nervous system with eight smaller brains controlling each of their eight tentacles. Two hearts pump blood to their gills, and one large heart distributes blood to other parts of the body. They can also camouflage themselves for protection when hunting for food and release toxic paint when alarmed.

Parrots are known for their extraordinary intelligence. They can solve puzzles and logical tasks. They learn from mistakes and draw conclusions from them. They use various available objects and tools to achieve a goal, such as getting treats. History knows parrots that could distinguish colors, answer questions and even ... were used in police investigations.

Check also:

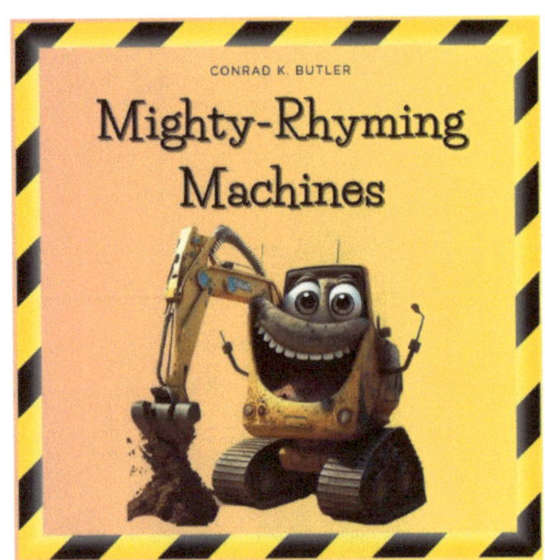

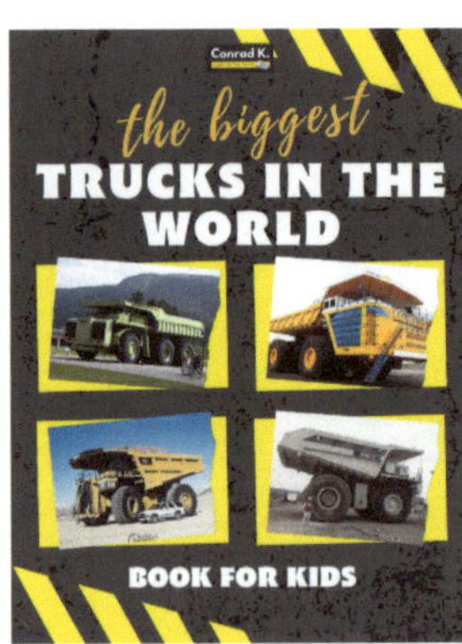

and much more!

www.ingramcontent.com/pod-product-compliance
Lightning Source LLC
LaVergne TN
LVHW071615180726
843512LV00003B/649